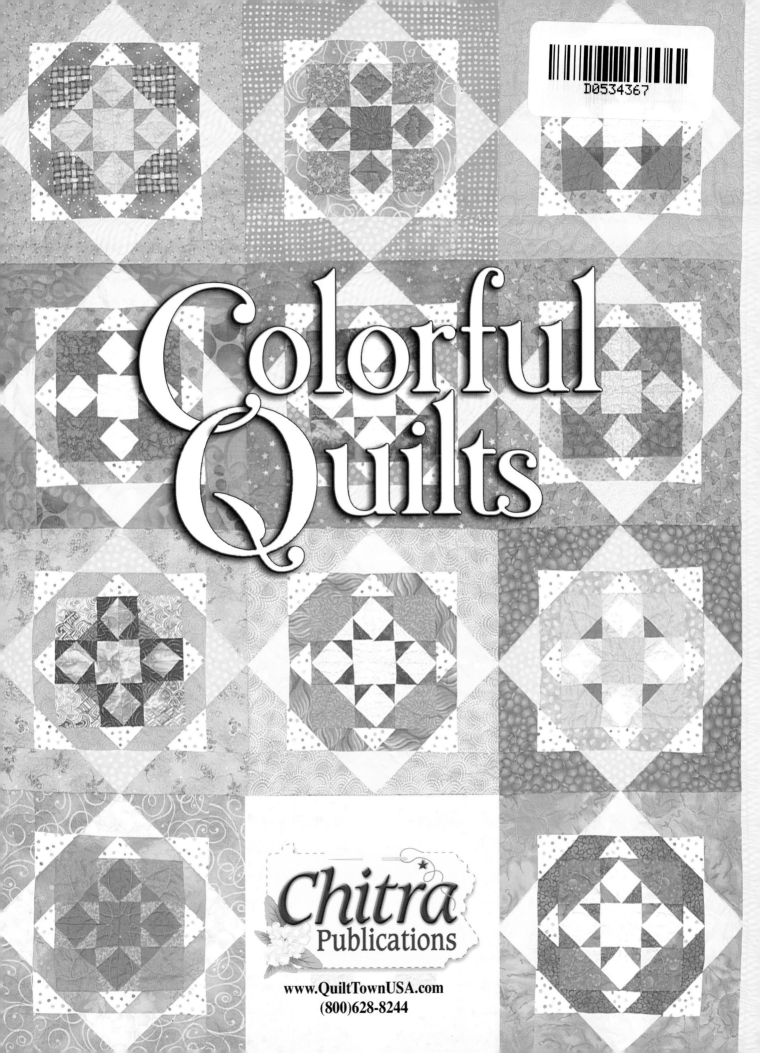

Colorful Quilts

Chitra Publications

www.QuiltTownUSA.com
(800)628-8244

D0534367

Copyright ©2004 Chitra Publications
All Right Reserved. Published in the United States of America.
Printed in China

Chitra Publications
2 Public Avenue
Montrose, Pennsylvania 18801-1220

No part of this publication may be reproduced or transmitted in any form or by any means, electronic or mechanical, including photocopy, recording, or any information storage and retrieval system now known or to be invented, without permission in writing from the publisher, except by a reviewer who wishes to quote brief passages in connection with a review written for inclusion in a magazine, newspaper, or broadcast.

First Printing 2004

Library of Congress Cataloging-in-Publication Data

Craig, Sharyn Squier, 1947-
    Colorful quilts / by Sharyn Craig, Christiane Meunier and others.
      p.cm.
    ISBN 1-885588-57-7
1. Patchwork—Patterns. 2. Quilting. 3. Patchwork quilts. I.
Meunier, Christiane. II. Title.
TT835.C71796 2004
746.46'041—dc22

                   2003025388

Edited by: Debra Feece, Deborah Hearn, and Pam Broe
Design and Illustrations: Brenda Pytlik
Photography: Van Zandbergen Photography, Brackney, Pennsylvania

Our Mission Statement:
We publish quality quilting magazines and books that recognize, promote, and inspire self-expression.
We are dedicated to serving our customers with respect, kindness, and efficiency.
www.QuiltTownUSA.com

Introduction

Do you remember when television was only black and white? For those who are too young to recall this, it probably is hard to imagine how fascinated we were to catch our first sight of a color TV. Yet both of us vividly recall the first time we ever saw one. Mesmerized by the moving colors that seemed to be floating inside that picture tube, we felt as if an entire movie theater had moved right into the living room!

Quiltmaking has rekindled our fascination with color in an even more exciting way. Unlike television viewing, it constantly requires our active participation. Choosing the perfect combination of fabrics and the best techniques to assemble them, we revel in the self-expression. Undoubtedly, of all the design elements, it is color that we enjoy most. Why, just arranging our fabric stashes in gradations of color is a pleasurable experience.

Being such good friends for many years, we've spent hours just talking about color! So along with quilts each of us have designed, we've chosen other ones that sing with color. If you happen to be in your sewing room, look around at all your wonderful fabrics and start thinking of which ones most closely match those in the projects ahead. Of course, you're likely to imagine some that would be an even better fit, giving you the perfect excuse to head to the fabric store! Whatever fabrics you choose, get ready, get set... sew!

Saying it in stitches,

Christiane

Sharyn

Contents

Alphabet Quilt

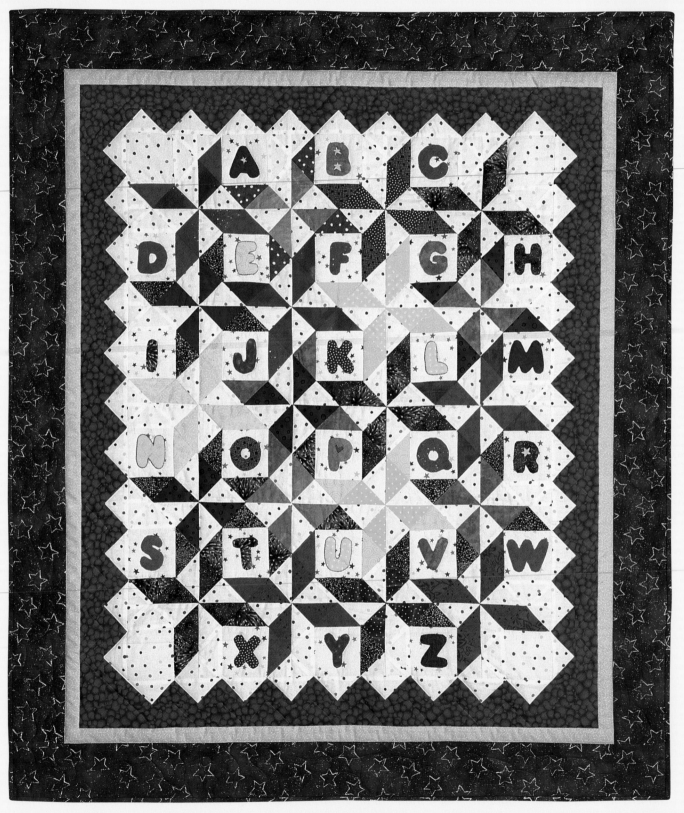

Sharyn stitched this adorable "**Alphabet Quilt**" with bright primary colors. It makes a great grandbaby quilt.

Materials

- Assorted bright prints in red, green, blue and yellow, totaling at least 5/8 yard
- 1 yard white print

NOTE: *If the following yellow and blue star prints are 44" wide, then borders can be cut crosswise. If not, either purchase 1 1/4 yards of each to cut borders lengthwise or piece crosswise strips to get the required length.*

- 3/4 yard red print, for the first border
- 3/8 yard yellow print, for the second border
- 1 yard blue star print, for the third border and binding
- 2 3/4 yards backing fabric
- 47" x 53" piece of batting
- Fusible web

Cutting

Appliqué patterns need to be enlarged by 200% and do not need a seam allowance. Reverse the enlarged patterns and trace around them on the paper side of the fusible web. Cut them out slightly beyond the traced line. Fuse them to the wrong side of the appropriate color scrap and cut them out on the line. All other dimensions include a 1/4" seam allowance.

For the Pinwheel blocks:

- Cut 10: 3" squares, bright red prints, in matching pairs
- Cut 10: 3" squares, bright green prints, in matching pairs
- Cut 6: 3" squares, bright yellow prints in matching pairs
- Cut 14: 3" squares, bright blue prints, in matching pairs

For the Square-in-a-square blocks:

- Cut 20: 2 5/8" squares, bright red prints
- Cut 20: 2 5/8" squares, bright green prints
- Cut 12: 2 5/8" squares, bright yellow prints
- Cut 28: 2 5/8" squares, bright blue prints

Also:

- Cut 40: 3" squares, white print
- Cut 18: 2 5/8" squares, white print
- Cut 30: 4 3/4" squares, white print
- Cut 9: 4 1/4" squares, red border print, then cut them in quarters diagonally to yield 36 small triangles
- Cut 2: 4" squares, red border print, then cut them in half diagonally to yield 4 large triangles
- Cut 4: 2 1/2" x 44" strips, red border print
- Cut 4: 1 1/2" x 44" strips, yellow border print
- Cut 4: 3 1/2" x 44" strips, blue star print
- Cut 5: 2 1/2" x 44" strips, blue star print, for the binding

Preparation

1. Draw a diagonal line from corner to corner on the wrong side of each 3" white print square and each 2 5/8" bright print square.

Directions

1. Following the manufacturer's directions, center and fuse the appliqué alphabet letters to 26 of the 4 3/4" white print squares, on point, as shown. Set them aside.

2. Lay a marked 3" white print square on a 3" red print square, right sides together, and sew 1/4" away from the diagonal line on both sides. Cut on the marked line to yield 2 pieced squares. Repeat, using a matching red print square.

3. Lay out the 4 pieced squares, as shown. Join them to complete a Pinwheel block. NOTE: *Make sure all your Pinwheel blocks spin in the same direction.*

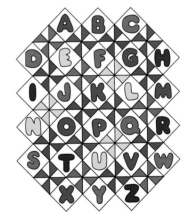

4. Make 5 red, 5 green, 7 blue, and 3 yellow Pinwheel blocks.

5. On a design wall or other flat surface at least 32" x 38", and referring to the quilt photo for color placement, lay out the pinwheels and the alphabet squares on point.

6. Remove the white print square with the letter E from the layout. Stitch marked red squares to the top and bottom corners of the square, as shown.

(Continued on page 28)

5

Batik
Courthouse Steps

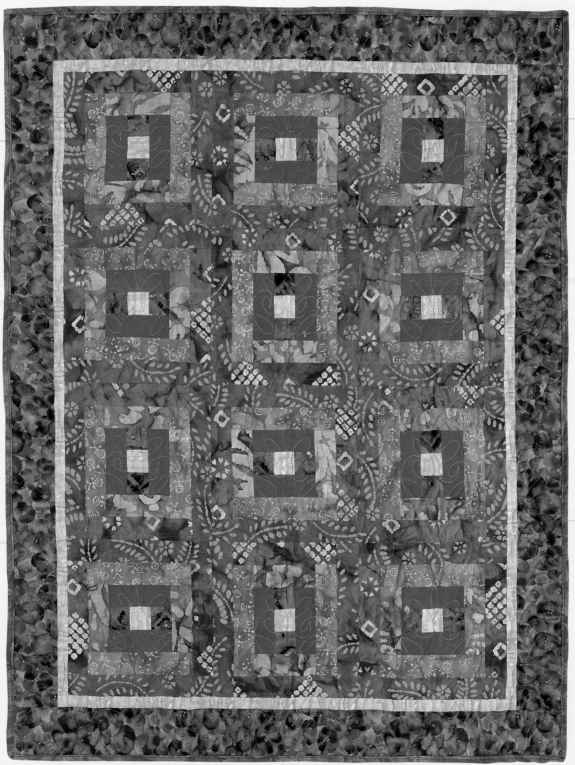

"Batik Courthouse Steps" is so easy to make. Christiane used some of her Batik fabric collection to create the bright and cheery look of this very traditional block.

Materials

- 1/2 yard gold print
- 1/2 yard purple print
- 1/4 yard red print
- 1/4 yard turquoise print
- 1/3 yard pink print
- 5/8 yard rose print
- 1 3/4 yards green print
- 2 1/2 yards backing fabric
- 44" x 55" piece of batting

Cutting

All dimensions include a 1/4" seam allowance. Cut the lengthwise strips before cutting smaller pieces from the same fabric.

For the blocks:
- Cut 12: 2" squares, gold print
- Cut 24: 2" x 8" strips, purple print
- Cut 24: 2" squares, purple print
- Cut 24: 2" x 5" strips, red print
- Cut 24: 2" x 5" strips, turquoise print
- Cut 24: 2" x 8" strips, pink print
- Cut 24: 2" x 11" strips, rose print

Also:
- Cut 2: 1 1/4" x 35" strips, gold print, for the inner border
- Cut 4: 1 1/4" x 25" strips, gold print, for the inner border
- Cut 2: 4" x 45" lengthwise strips, green print, for the outer border
- Cut 2: 4" x 42" lengthwise strips, green print, for the outer border
- Cut 6: 2 1/2" x 40" strips, green print, for the binding

Directions

1. Stitch a 2" gold print square between two 2" purple print squares to make a pieced strip, as shown.

2. Stitch the pieced strip between two 2" x 5" red print strips to make a pieced square, as shown.

3. Stitch the pieced square between two 2" x 5" turquoise print strips.

4. Stitch the pieced unit between two 2" x 8" pink print strips.

5. Stitch the pieced square between two 2" x 8" purple print strips as shown.

6. Stitch the pieced unit between two 2" x 11" rose print strips to complete a Log Cabin block, as shown. Make 12.

Assembly

1. Lay out the blocks in 4 rows of 3.

2. Stitch the blocks into rows. Join the rows.

3. Stitch two 1 1/4" x 25" gold print strips together, end to end, to make a pieced border strip. Make 2.

4. Measure the length of the quilt. Trim the pieced border strips to that measurement and stitch them to the long sides of the quilt.

5. Measure the width of the quilt, including the borders. Trim the 1 1/4" x 35" gold print strips to that measurement and stitch them to the remaining sides of the quilt.

6. In the same manner, trim the 4" x 45" green print strips to fit the quilt's length and stitch them to the long sides of the quilt.

7. Trim the 4" x 42" green print strips to fit the quilt's width and stitch them to the remaining sides of the quilt.

8. Finish the quilt as described in the *General Directions,* using the 2 1/2" x 40" green print strips for the binding. ◆

Bright Lattice

Caitlin Feece of Montrose, Pennsylvania, chose the wild fabrics for **"Bright Lattice"** and her mom, Debra, made the quilt. It was Debra's first attempt at quilting on a long arm quilting machine. She says, "It looks pretty good if you don't look too closely!"

Materials

- Fat quarter (18" x 20") each of 12 assorted bright prints
- 2 yards white print
- 1 1/2 yards red
- 4 yards backing fabric
- 68" square of batting

Cutting

Dimensions include a 1/4" seam allowance. Cut the lengthwise red strips before cutting other pieces from that yardage.

- Cut 80: 2" x 18" strips, assorted bright prints
- Cut 41: 6 1/2" squares, white print
- Cut 4: 9 3/4" squares, white print, then cut them in quarters diagonally to yield 16 setting triangles
- Cut 2: 5 1/8" squares, white print, then cut them in half diagonally to yield 4 corner triangles
- Cut 6: 2 1/2" x 52" lengthwise strips, red, for the binding
- Cut 40: 3 1/2" squares, red
- Cut 5: 5 1/2" squares, red, then cut them in quarters diagonally to yield 20 setting triangles

Directions

1. Sew four 2" x 18" bright print strips together along their length to make a panel. Make 20. Press all seam allowances in the same direction.

2. Cut five 3 1/2" sections from each panel.

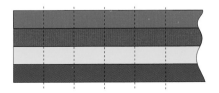

3. Sew 2 sections to each of twenty-five 6 1/2" white print squares, as shown. Press the seam allowances toward the squares.

Assembly

4. Referring to the Assembly Diagram, sew the pieced units and remaining 6 1/2" white print squares into diagonal rows.

5. Sew the white print setting triangles to the ends of the rows. Press the seam allowances toward the squares and triangles.

6. Sew the 3 1/2" red squares and remaining sections together to make sashings. Sew the red triangles to the ends of the sashings. Press the seam allowances toward the squares and triangles.

7. Join the rows and sashing strips.

8. Sew a pieced unit and red triangles to the remaining corners.

9. Sew the white print corner triangles to the corners of the quilt.

10. Finish the quilt as described in the *General Directions*, using the 2 1/2" x 52" red strips for the binding. ◆

Assembly Diagram

Christiana's Quilt

Judi Drozdowski of Grand Island, New York, made **"Christiana's Quilt"** for the first child of her friend Karen, whom she's known since they were four-years old. Judi chose primary colors to match the special baby's nursery. We're sure this cheerful quilt will be treasured for many years to come.

Materials

- 3/8 yard each of 5 bright prints and solids for the Star blocks
- 3/4 yard blue
- 1/2 yard light print
- 1 1/4 yards white
- 1 1/2 yards backing fabric
- 40" x 46" piece of batting

Cutting

For each of 21 Star blocks:

- Cut 1: 3 1/2" square, bright print or solid
- Cut 8: 2" squares, same bright print or solid

Also:

- Cut 42: 3 1/2" squares, light print
- Cut 5: 2" x 40" strips, blue
- Cut 5: 2" x 40" strips, white
- Cut 84: 2" squares, white
- Cut 84: 2" x 3 1/2" rectangles, white
- Cut 5: 2 1/2" x 40" strips, blue, for the binding

Directions

For each Star block:

1. Draw a diagonal line from corner to corner on the wrong side of each 2" bright print or solid square.

2. Place a marked 2" square on one end of a 2" x 3 1/2" white rectangle, right sides together. Sew on the drawn line. Press the square toward the corner, aligning the raw edges. Trim the seam allowance to 1/4".

3. Place a marked square on the opposite end of the white rectangle. Sew, press and trim, as before to complete a Star point unit. Make 4.

4. Lay out the 4 Star point units, a matching 3 1/2" bright square, and four 2" white squares. Sew them into rows, as shown. Join the rows to complete a block. Make 21. Set them aside.

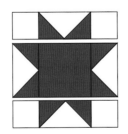

5. Sew a 2" x 40" blue strip to a 2" x 40" white strip, right sides together along their length, to make a pieced panel. Make 5. Press the seam allowances toward the blue strips.

6. Cut eighty-four 2" segments from the pieced panels.

7. Join 2 segments to make a Four Patch. Make 42.

8. Lay out 2 Four Patches and two 3 1/2" light print squares. Sew them into rows and join the rows to make a Chain block. Make 21.

Assembly

1. Referring to the quilt photo, lay out the Star blocks and Chain blocks in 7 rows of 6.

2. Sew the blocks into rows and join the rows.

3. Finish the quilt as described in the *General Directions*, using the 2 1/2" x 40" blue strips for the binding. ◆

Country Roads

What better way to showcase colorful fabrics than in this timeless design called **"Country Roads."** White shirting strips create the illusion of scrappy blocks. But look closely, the white strips actually make a plus sign through each block. Dark squares criss-cross diagonally to make another graphic display.

Materials

- Assorted dark prints totaling at least 4 yards
- Assorted light prints totaling at least 1 3/4 yards
- 3 3/4 yards light stripe
- 5 1/2 yards backing fabric
- 79" x 93" piece of batting

Cutting

Dimensions include a 1/4" seam allowance. Group the pieces for each block as you cut them.

For each of 30 blocks:
- Cut 13: 2 1/2" squares, dark print
- Cut 4: 4 1/8" squares, light print; then cut each in quarters diagonally
- Cut 4: 4 7/8" squares, second dark print; then cut each in half diagonally

Also:
- Cut 9: 2 1/2" x 94" lengthwise strips, light stripe; then cut fourteen 6 1/2"-long strips from each for a total of 126 sashing strips. You will use 120.
- Cut 2: 2 1/2" x 94" lengthwise strips, light stripe, for the border

- Cut 2: 2 1/2" x 79" strips, light stripe, for the border
- Cut 2 1/2"-wide bias strips, light stripe, totaling at least 340" when joined for the binding

Directions

For each block:

1. Sew a light print triangle to a 2 1/2" dark print square to make Unit 1, as shown. Make 8. Press the seam allowances toward the dark print squares. Set them aside.

2. Sew light print triangles to a 2 1/2" dark print square to make Unit 2, as shown. Make 4. Press the seam allowances toward the dark print squares.

3. Lay out 2 Unit 1's and a Unit 2. Join them to make a pieced unit. Make 4.

4. Sew dark print triangles to a pieced unit to make a corner unit. Make 4.

5. Lay out 4 corner units, a 2 1/2" dark print square and four 2 1/2" x 6 1/2" stripe sashing strips, as shown.

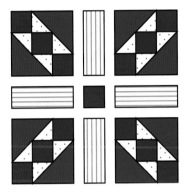

6. Sew the units into rows and join the rows to make a block. Make 30.

Assembly

1. Referring to the photo, lay out the blocks in 6 rows of 5.

2. Sew the blocks into rows and join the rows.

3. Center and sew the 2 1/2" x 79" stripe strips to the top and bottom of the quilt. Start and stop stitching 1/4" from the edges and backstitch.

4. Center and sew the 2 1/2" x 94" stripe strips to the sides of the quilt in the same manner.

5. Miter the corners as described in the *General Directions*.

6. Finish the quilt as described in the *General Directions*. Use the 2 1/2"-wide light stripe bias strips for the binding. ◆

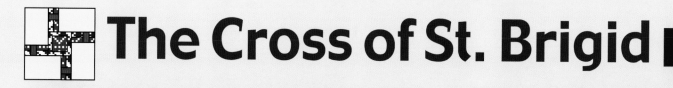

The Cross of St. Brigid

Christiane was inspired by the legend of St. Brigid and *The Book of Kells*, when she created her stunning quilt, **"The Cross of St. Brigid."** This fun and colorful quilt is easy to make using the partial seam technique.

Materials

- Fat quarter (18" x 20") each of 20 assorted yellow and gold prints
- Fat eighth (10" x 18") each of 10 assorted orange and red prints
- Fat eighth each of 10 assorted teal and green prints
- Fat quarter each of 6 assorted blue and purple prints
- 2 3/4 yards dark purple print, for the inner and outer borders and binding
- 5 1/2 yards backing fabric
- 84" x 96" piece of batting

Cutting

Dimensions include a 1/4" seam allowance.

- Cut 120: 4 1/2" x 6 1/2" rectangles, yellow or gold print
- Cut 10: 1 1/2" x 18" strips, yellow or gold print, for the middle border
- Cut 120: 1 1/2" x 2 1/2" rectangles, orange or red print
- Cut 10: 1 1/2" x 18" strips, orange or red print, for the middle border
- Cut 4: 2 1/2" squares, red print, for the middle border corners
- Cut 30: 2 1/2" squares, teal or green print
- Cut 40: 1 1/2" x 18" strips, teal or green print, for the blocks and middle border
- Cut 70: 1 1/2" x 18" strips, blue or purple print, for the blocks and middle border
- Cut 4: 2 1/2" x 76" lengthwise

strips, dark purple print, for the inner border
- Cut 4: 5" x 96" lengthwise strips, dark purple, for the outer border
- Cut 4: 2 1/2" x 98" lengthwise strips, dark purple print, for the binding

Directions

For each of 30 blocks:

1. Select a 2 1/2" teal or green print square, a matching 1 1/2" x 18" teal or green print strip, two 1 1/2" x 18" same blue or purple print strips, and four 1 1/2" x 2 1/2" same orange or red print rectangles.

2. Cut two 2 1/2" lengths from a blue or purple print strip and stitch them to opposite sides of the teal or green print square as shown.

3. Cut two 4 1/2" lengths from the blue or purple print strips and stitch them to the remaining sides of the square to make a center unit.

4. Stitch the remaining 1 1/2" x 18" blue or purple print strip to the 1 1/2" x 18" teal or green print strip, right sides together along their length, to make a pieced panel. Cut four 1 1/2" slices and four 2 1/2" slices from the pieced panel, as shown.

5. Stitch a 1 1/2" x 2 1/2" orange or red print rectangle between a 1 1/2" and a 2 1/2" length from the pieced panel to make a pieced rectangle, as shown. Make 4.

6. Stitch a pieced rectangle to one end of a 4 1/2" x 6 1/2" yellow or gold print rectangle, carefully positioning the pieced rectangle as shown, to make a side unit. Make 4.

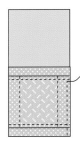

7. Stitch the center square to a side unit, starting about 1" from the top of the center square and stitching all the way to the bottom.

8. Stitch a side unit to the right side of the pieced section, as shown.

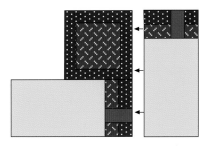

(Continued on page 29)

Dawn of a New Era

Lisa Konkel of Garfield, New Jersey, gave a new look to traditional Sawtooth Star blocks. Special batik, hand-dyed, and marbled fabrics provide a burst of color in **"Dawn of a New Era."** Make a quilt like Lisa's using your favorite bright fabrics.

Materials
- Assorted bright batiks, marbled, and hand-dyed fabrics including purple, blue, green, red, orange, and yellow
- 3/4 yard dark fabric for the binding
- 4 1/8 yards backing fabric
- 63" x 72" piece of batting

Cutting

Refer to the photo for color placement. You may want to cut the pieces for the blocks from appropriate fabrics as you go along.

For each of seventy 3" Star blocks:
- Cut 8: 1 1/4" squares, one bright fabric for the star
- Cut 1: 2" square, same star fabric
- Cut 4: 1 1/4" x 2" rectangles, one bright fabric for the background
- Cut 4: 1 1/4" squares, same background fabric

For each of sixty-four 6" Star blocks:
- Cut 8: 2" squares, one bright fabric for the star
- Cut 1: 3 1/2" square, same star fabric
- Cut 4: 2" x 3 1/2" rectangles, one bright fabric for the background
- Cut 4: 2" squares, same background print

For each of three 12" Star blocks:
- Cut 8: 2" squares, one bright print for the center star
- Cut 1: 3 1/2" square, same star fabric
- Cut 8: 3 1/2" squares, one bright fabric for the large star
- Cut 4: 2" x 3 1/2" rectangles, same large star fabric

- Cut 4: 2" squares, same large star fabric
- Cut 4: 3 1/2" x 6 1/2" rectangles, one bright fabric for the background
- Cut 4: 3 1/2" squares, same background fabric

Also:
- Cut 44: 3 1/2" squares, assorted bright fabrics
- Cut 13: 5 1/2" squares, assorted bright fabrics, then cut them in quarters diagonally to yield 52 small triangles
- Cut 2: 5 1/8" squares, assorted bright fabrics, then cut them in half diagonally to yield 4 corner triangles
- Cut 7: 2 1/2" x 40" strips, dark binding fabric

Directions

For each 3" (finished size) Star block:
1. Draw a diagonal line from corner to corner on the wrong side of each 1 1/4" star fabric square.
2. Place a marked square on one end of a 1 1/4" x 2" background rectangle, right sides together. Sew on the drawn line, as shown.
3. Press the square toward the corner, aligning the edges. Trim the seam allowance to 1/4".
4. Place a marked square on the opposite end of the rectangle, right sides together. Sew on the drawn line. Press and trim, as before, to complete a Star Point unit. Make 4.

5. Lay out the Star Point units, the 2" bright square, and the four matching 1 1/4" background squares. Sew them into rows and join the rows to complete the block. Make 70.

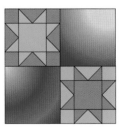

For each 6" Star block:
1. Make 64 blocks in the same manner, using the pieces cut for those blocks.

For each 12" Star block:
1. Make a 6" Star block, as before.
2. Make 4 large Star Point units using the 3 1/2" x 6 1/2" background rectangles and the 3 1/2" large star squares.
3. Lay out the 6" center block, the large Star Point units, and the 3 1/2" background squares. Sew them into rows and join the rows to complete the block. Make 3.

Assembly

1. Lay out the 12" Star blocks, 6" Star blocks, 3" Star blocks, the 3 1/2" bright squares, and the small triangles in diagonal rows, as shown in the Assembly Diagram (page 29). Rearrange the blocks until you like the color placement.
2. Sew two 3" Star blocks and two 3 1/2" bright squares together to make a Four Patch block, as shown. Make 22. Place them back into the layout.

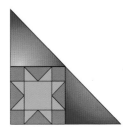

3. Sew 2 small triangles to a 3" Star block to make a setting triangle. Make 26. Place them back into the layout.

(Continued on page 29)

Kaufman's Waterwheel

Candy Huddleston of Spokane, Washington, used bright hand-dyed-look prints to create **"Kaufman's Waterwheel."** Christiane and Sharyn really like the look of Candy's quilt, especially the "piano-key" border that adds rhythm to the diagonal movement of the blocks.

Materials

- Fat quarter (18" x 20") each of 12 brights
- 1 yard yellow
- Fat quarter each of 12 lights
- 1/2 yard blue for the binding
- 4 1/2 yards backing fabric
- 61" square of batting

Cutting

Dimensions include a 1/4" seam allowance.

- Cut 2: 2" x 20" strips from each of 12 brights
- Cut 4: 3 7/8" squares from each of 12 brights
- Cut 2: 3 1/2" squares from each of 12 brights
- Cut 8: 2" x 25" strips, yellow, for the inner border
- Cut 12: 2" x 20" strips, yellow
- Cut 2: 3 7/8" squares, yellow
- Cut 1: 3 1/2" square, yellow
- Cut 4: 4 1/2" squares, yellow, for the border corners
- Cut 3: 2" x 20" strips from each of 12 lights
- Cut 4: 3 7/8" squares, from each of 12 lights
- Cut 2: 3 7/8" matching light squares, for the yellow block
- Cut 6: 2 1/2" x 40" strips, blue, for the binding

Preparation

1. Draw a diagonal line from corner to corner on the wrong side of each 3 7/8" light square.

Directions

1. Stitch a 2" x 20" yellow strip to a 2" x 20" light strip, right sides together along their length, to make a pieced panel. Repeat, using yellow with each of the light colors for a total of 12 pieced panels.

2. Cut one hundred four 2" yellow/light slices from the pieced panels (8 or 9 from each color), as shown. Set them aside.

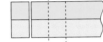

3. In the same manner, stitch each 2" x 20" bright strip to a remaining 2" x 20" light strip. Set one panel from each color aside.

4. Cut eight 2" bright/light slices from each remaining pieced panel for a total of 96. Group them by color and set them aside.

For each Waterwheel block:

1. Stitch a bright/light slice and a yellow/light slice into a Four Patch, as shown. Make 4 using the same colors. Set them aside.

2. Lay a 3 7/8" marked light square on a 3 7/8" bright square, right sides together. Stitch 1/4" away from the diagonal line on both sides, as shown. Make 2.

3. Cut on the drawn lines to yield 4 pieced squares. Press the seam allowances toward the bright.

4. Lay out the Four Patches, pieced squares, and a 3 1/2" matching bright square in 3 rows of 3. Stitch them into rows and join the rows to complete a

Waterwheel block. Make 2 from each bright color.

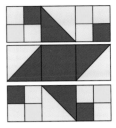

5. In the same manner, make one yellow Waterwheel block.

Assembly

1. Referring to the quilt photo, lay out the Waterwheel blocks in 5 rows of 5.

2. Stitch the blocks into rows and join the rows.

3. Stitch two 2" x 25" yellow strips together, end to end to make a pieced border. Make 4.

4. Measure the length of the quilt. Trim two pieced borders to that measurement. Stitch them to opposite sides of the quilt.

5. Measure the width of the quilt, including the borders. Trim the remaining pieced borders to that measurement. Stitch them to the remaining sides of the quilt.

6. From the remaining bright/light pieced panels, cut sixty-four 4 1/2" slices. Include at least four slices from the yellow/light pieced panel scraps.

7. Stitch 16 slices together, to make an outer border. Make 4.

8. Stitch outer borders to 2 opposite sides of the quilt.

9. Stitch a 4 1/2" yellow square to each end of the remaining outer borders, to make a long border.

10. Stitch the long borders to the remaining sides of the quilt.

11. Finish the quilt as described in the *General Directions*, using the 2 1/2" x 40" blue strips for the binding. ◆

New York Beauty
A Variation in Jellies

This striking **"New York Beauty: A Variation in Jellies"** is an original design of Lisa O'Neill of Exton, Pennsylvania, and was quilted by Barbara Persing of Frederick, Pennsylvania. The wonderful use of colors makes this quilt one you are sure to want to stitch.

Materials
- Assorted fat quarters (18" x 20"), bright and dark fabrics, totaling at least 6 yards
- 1/2 yard bright yellow
- 1/4 yard black
- 1/4 yard light gray
- 5/8 yard pink-orange for the binding
- Paper for the foundations

Cutting
Foundation H and the Corner Block foundation (page 30) need to be enlarged 200% and do not include a seam allowance. Fabric for foundation piecing will be cut as you stitch the blocks. Each piece should be at least 1/2" larger on all sides than the section it will cover. Refer to the General Directions *as needed. Patterns for A through G, J, and K are full size and include a 1/4" seam allowance, as do all dimensions given.*

From assorted dark fabrics:
- Cut 4: A
- Cut 4: AR
- Cut 12: C
- Cut 48: D
- Cut 20: F
- Cut 12: G

From assorted bright fabrics:
- Cut 12: A
- Cut 12: AR
- Cut 20: B
- Cut 20: BR
- Cut 48: each E and ER
- Cut 20: G

Also:
- Cut 4: 1 1/2" x 40" strips, black
- Cut 4: 1 1/2" x 40" strips, light gray
- Cut 4: C, bright yellow
- Cut 12: F, bright yellow
- Cut 4: each J and K, bright yellow
- Cut 16: 1 7/8" squares, dark fabric

- Cut 8: 2 1/2" x 40" pink/orange strips, for the binding

Directions
Follow the foundation-piecing instructions in General Directions *to piece the blocks.*

1. Trace enlarged patterns on the foundation paper, transferring all lines and numbers. Cut each foundation out on the outer line. Make 36 H's and 4 Corner Blocks.

2. Piece the foundations in numerical order using the following fabrics in these positions:

For 4 H foundations:
> 1, 3, 5, 7, 9, 11, 13, 15, 17, 19 - orange
> 2, 4, 6, 8, 10, 12, 14, 16, 18 - darks

For 12 H foundations:
> 1, 3, 5, 7, 9, 11, 13, 15, 17, 19 - bright yellow
> 2, 4, 6, 8, 10, 12, 14, 16, 18 - darks

For 20 H foundations:
> 1, 3, 5, 7, 9, 11, 13, 15, 17, 19 - one fabric
> 2, 4, 6, 8, 10, 12, 14, 16, 18 - contrasting fabric

For 4 Corner Blocks:
> 1 - orange
> 2, 3 - blue
> 4, 5 - orange
> 6, 7 - blue

3. Trim the fabric 1/4" beyond the edges of each foundation.

4. Stitch a bright yellow K to the inner corner of each corner block as shown. Set them aside.

5. Sew a bright yellow J and a bright orange H together, as shown, easing the 2 curved seams. Press the seam allowances

toward H. Make 4.

6. Sew a bright yellow C between a dark A and a dark AR. Make 4.

7. Sew a unit to the outer curve of an H/J unit, clipping the inner curve of A/C/AR where necessary. Make 4. Set them aside for the center.

8. Lay out a bright yellow F, a dark G, a bright yellow H, a bright A, a bright AR and a dark C. Stitch them together. Make 12.

9. Lay out a dark F, a bright G, an H, a bright B, and a bright BR. Stitch them together. Make 20. Set 4 aside for the inner corner blocks.

10. Lay a 1 7/8" dark square on the corner opposite F. Stitch across the square diagonally, as shown.

11. Press the square toward the corner, aligning the edges. Trim the seam allowance to 1/4". Make 16 blocks in this manner.

Assembly
1. Referring to the quilt photo, lay out the blocks in 6 rows of 6. Stitch the blocks into rows and join the rows.

(Continued on page 30)

Pinwheels on Parade

Sharyn's cheerful **"Pinwheels on Parade"** is the perfect size for that special toddler. It's a great way to show off your wonderful fabric stash.

Materials

For the Pinwheel blocks:

- Purple print square at least 5 3/4"
- 1/4 yard each, orange and yellow prints
- 3/8 yard each, lime, pink, and turquoise prints

For the Alternate squares:

- 1/4 yard each, in purple, orange, yellow, lime, pink and turquoise prints

Also:

- 1 1/8 yards white print
- 1 1/8 yards border print
- Pink print at least 8" square for the cornerstones
- 3/8 yard pink print for the binding
- 2 1/2 yards backing fabric
- 40" x 48" piece of batting

Cutting

Dimensions include a 1/4" seam allowance.

For the Pinwheel blocks:

- Cut 1: 5 3/4" square, purple print
- Cut 2: 5 3/4" squares, orange print
- Cut 3: 5 3/4" squares, yellow print
- Cut 4: 5 3/4" squares, lime print
- Cut 4: 5 3/4" squares, pink print
- Cut 4: 5 3/4" squares, turquoise print

For the Alternate squares:

- Cut 4: 4 1/2" squares, purple print
- Cut 6: 4 1/2" squares, orange print
- Cut 4: 4 1/2" squares, yellow print
- Cut 4: 4 1/2" squares, lime print
- Cut 6: 4 1/2" squares, pink print
- Cut 7: 4 1/2" squares, turquoise print

Also:

- Cut 18: 5 3/4" squares, white print
- Cut 4: 4" x 38" lengthwise strips, border print
- Cut 4: 4" squares, pink print, for the cornerstones
- Cut 5: 2 1/2" x 40" strips, pink print, for the binding

Directions

For the Pinwheel blocks:

1. Draw diagonal lines from corner to corner on the wrong side of each 5 3/4" white print square. Draw horizontal and vertical lines through the centers.

2. Place a marked white print square on a 5 3/4" purple print square, right sides together. Stitch 1/4" away from the diagonal lines on both sides.

3. Cut the squares on the drawn lines to yield 8 pieced squares. Press the seam allowances toward the purple print.

4. Lay out 4 pieced squares in 2 rows of 2. Stitch the squares into rows. Join the rows to make a Pinwheel block, as shown. You will have 4 pieced squares left over.

5. In the same manner, make 4 orange, 5 yellow, 7 lime, 7 pink, and 8 turquoise Pinwheels.

Assembly

1. Referring to the quilt photo, lay out the 4 1/2" print squares and the Pinwheel blocks in 9 rows of 7.

2. Stitch the blocks into row and join the rows.

3. Measure the length of the quilt. Trim 2 of the 4" x 38" border print strips to that measurement.

4. Stitch a trimmed strip between two 4" third pink print squares to make a pieced border. Make 2.

5. Measure the width of the quilt. Trim the remaining two 4" x 38" border print strips to that measurement and stitch them to the top of bottom of the quilt.

6. Stitch the pieced borders to the sides of the quilt.

7. Finish the quilt according to the *General Directions,* using the 2 1/2" x 40" pink print strips for the binding. ◆

Ring Around the "G" Block

Sharyn took some "so-so" blocks and perked them up with bright primary colors for **"Ring Around the "G" Block."** This is a great quilt for any child's room.

Materials

- Assorted light prints, each at least 7" square and totaling at least 1/2 yard
- Assorted bright prints, each at least 10" x 11" and totaling at least 2 yards
- 1/2 yard light polka dot print
- 12 yellow prints, each at least 4 1/2" x 10"
- 3/4 yard yellow print for the border and binding
- 2 1/2 yards backing fabric
- 44" x 56" piece of batting

Cutting

Dimensions include a 1/4" seam allowance.

For each of 12 blocks:

- Cut 5: 2 1/2" squares, one light print
- Cut 4: 1 1/2" squares, same light print
- Cut 16: 1 1/2" squares, first bright print
- Cut 4: 2 1/2" squares, second bright print
- Cut 4: 1 1/2" x 4 1/2" strips, third bright print
- Cut 4: 1 1/2" x 3 1/2" strips, third bright print
- Cut 4: 2 1/2" x 6 1/2" strips, fourth bright print
- Cut 4: 2 1/2" x 4 1/2" strips, fourth bright print
- Cut 4: 2 1/2" x 4 1/2" strips, one yellow print

Also:

- Cut 48: 1 1/2" x 2 1/2" rectangles, light polka dot
- Cut 48: 2 1/2" squares, light polka dot
- Cut 5: 2 1/2" x 40" strips, yellow print, for the binding
- Cut 5: 2" x 40" strips, yellow print, for the borders

Directions

For each block:

1. Draw a line from corner to corner on the wrong side of each 1 1/2" bright square and each 1 1/2" light square.

2. Place marked bright squares on opposite corners of a 2 1/2" light print square, right sides together. Sew on the drawn lines, as shown.

3. Press the squares toward the corners, aligning the edges. Trim the seam allowances to 1/4".

4. Place bright squares on the remaining corners of the light square. Stitch, press, and trim as before to complete a Square-in-a-square. Make 4.

5. In the same manner, sew a marked 1 1/2" light square on one corner of each 2 1/2" second bright square to make corner squares.

6. Lay out the corner squares, Square-in-a-square units, and 2 1/2" light square. Sew them into rows and join the rows to make the center section. Set it aside.

7. Place a 1 1/2" x 3 1/2" third bright strip on a 1 1/2" x 2 1/2" light polka dot strip, right sides together. Sew from corner to corner, as shown. Press the seam allowance toward the bright strip, then trim it to 1/4".

8. Place a 1 1/2" x 3 1/2" third bright strip on the other end of the polka dot strip. Sew from corner to corner. Press and trim. Make 2.

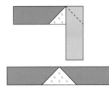

9. In the same manner, make 2 strips using 1 1/2" x 2 1/2" light polka dot strips and the 1 1/2" x 4 1/2" third bright strips.

10. Sew the short strips to opposite sides of the center section. Sew the long strips to the remaining sides.

11. Draw a diagonal line from corner to corner on the wrong side of each 2 1/2" light polka dot square.

12. Place a marked square on one corner of the block right sides together. Sew on the drawn line. Press the square toward the corner, aligning the edges. Trim the underneath layers, leaving a 1/4" seam allowance. Repeat for the remaining corners.

13. Make 2 pieced strips as before, using 2 1/2" x 4 1/2" yellow print strips and 2 1/2" x 4 1/2" fourth bright strips.

(Continued on page 27)

Twyla's Quilt

To complement as well as brighten up the decor of Twyla Estell's office, Christiane used a wide variety of batiks in **"Twyla's Quilt."**

Materials

- 1/2 yard each of 14 assorted prints or assorted print scraps totaling 7 yards
- 2/3 yard of print fabric for the binding
- 5 yards backing fabric
- 81" x 92" piece of batting

Cutting

All dimensions include a 1/4" seam allowance.

For each of 56 blocks:

- Cut 1: 4 1/2" square, print
- Cut 2: 3" x 4 1/2" strips, contrasting print
- Cut 2: 3" x 9 1/2" strips, same contrasting print
- Cut 2: 1 1/2" x 9 1/2" strips, second contrasting print
- Cut 2: 1 1/2" x 11 1/2" strips, second contrasting print

Also:

- Cut 9: 2 1/2" x 40" strips, print, for the binding

Directions

1. Stitch the 4 1/2" square between two 3" x 4 1/2" contrasting print strips to make a pieced unit, as shown.

2. Stitch a pieced unit between two 3" x 9 1/2" contrasting print strips to make a pieced square.

3. Stitch the pieced square between two 1 1/2" x 9 1/2" contrasting print strips as shown.

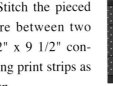

4. Stitch the pieced unit between two 1 1/2" x 11 1/2" contrasting print strips to complete a Framed block, as shown. Make 56.

Assembly

1. Lay out the blocks in 8 rows of 7.
2. Stitch the blocks into rows. Join the rows.
3. Finish the quilt according to the *General Directions*, using the 2 1/2" x 40" print strips for the binding. ◆

Ring Around the "G" Block
(continued from page 25)

14. Make 2 pieced strips using the remaining 2 1/2" x 4 1/2" yellow print strips and the 2 1/2" x 6 1/2" fourth bright strips.

15. Sew the short pieced strips to opposite sides of the block. Sew the long pieced strips to the remaining sides to complete the block. Make 12.

Assembly

1. Lay out the blocks in 4 rows of 3. Sew the blocks into rows and join the rows.

2. Cut one 2" x 40" yellow print strip into two 20" lengths. Sew one 20" length to each of two 2" x 40" yellow print strips.

3. Measure the length of the quilt. Trim the pieced strips to that measurement. Sew them to the long sides of the quilt.

4. Measure the width of the quilt, including the borders. Trim the remaining 2" x 40" yellow print strips to that measurement. Sew them to the remaining sides of the quilt.

5. Finish the quilt as described in the *General Directions*, using the 2 1/2" x 40" yellow print strips for the binding. ◆

Alphabet Quilt
(continued from page 5)

7. Press the red squares toward the corners and trim the seam allowances to 1/4".

8. Stitch a marked blue square to the left side of the "E" square and a marked green square to the right side. Press and trim as before to complete a Square-in-a-square block. Return it to the layout.

9. Referring to the photo as necessary, stitch appropriately colored squares to the corners of the remaining letter squares. The outer letter squares only have colored squares on 2 corners. The corner white print squares have a colored square on one corner.

10. Stitch the blocks into diagonal rows, but do not join the rows yet. Return the rows to the layout.

11. Stitch small red print triangles to adjacent sides of a 2 5/8" white print square to complete a triangle unit. Make 18.

12. Referring to the quilt photo, place the triangle units along the edges of the layout. Place a large red print triangle in each corner.

13. Stitch the triangle units and large red print triangles to the diagonal rows. Join the rows.

14. Measure the length of the quilt. Trim two 2 1/2" x 44" red print strips to that measurement and stitch them to the long sides of the quilt.

15. Measure the width of the quilt, including the borders. Trim the remaining 2 1/2" x 44" red print strips to that measurement and stitch them to the

remaining sides of the quilt.

16. In the same manner, trim 2 of the 1 1/2" x 44" yellow print strips to fit the quilt's length and stitch them to the long sides of the quilt.

17. Trim the remaining 1 1/2" x 44" yellow print strips to fit the quilt's width, including the borders, and stitch them to the remaining sides of the quilt.

18. Trim 2 of the 3 1/2" x 44" blue print strips to fit the quilt's length and stitch them to the long sides of the quilt.

19. Trim the remaining 3 1/2" x 44" blue print strips to fit the quilt's width, including the borders, and stitch them to the remaining sides of the quilt.

20. Stitch around the alphabet pieces with a machine zigzag or buttonhole stitch.

21. Finish the quilt as described in the *General Directions,* using the 2 1/2" x 44" blue print strips for the binding. ◆

Patterns for Alphabet Quilt
(Instructions begin on page 4—Enlarge letters at 200%—Full-Size Appliqué Patterns are available on our website www.QuiltTownUSA.com)

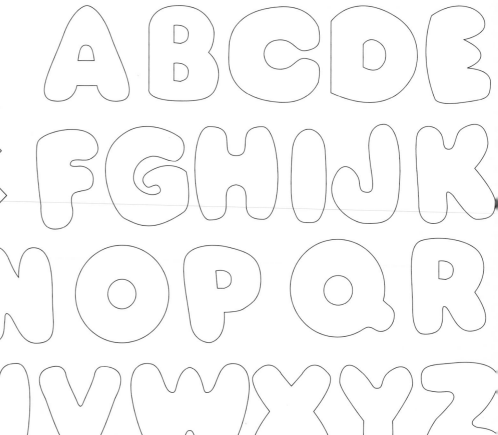

The Cross of St. Brigid
(continued from page 15)

9. Stitch a side unit to the top, then another side unit to the left side.

10. Finish stitching the partial seam to complete the block.

Assembly

1. Referring to the quilt photo, lay out the blocks in 6 rows of 5. Stitch the blocks into rows and join the rows.
2. Measure the length of the quilt. Trim two of the 2 1/2" x 76" dark purple print strips to that measurement and stitch them to the long sides of the quilt.
3. Measure the width of the quilt including the borders. Trim the remaining 2 1/2" x 76" dark purple print strips to that measurement and stitch them to the remaining sides of the quilt.
4. Alternating colors, stitch 8 of the remaining 1 1/2" x 18" print strips, right sides together along their length, to make a pieced panel. Make 5.

5. Cut seven 2 1/2" slices from each pieced panel for a total of 35.

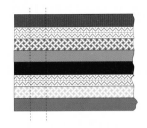

6. Lay out 8 slices. Stitch them together, end to end, to make a short middle border. Make 2.
7. Stitch a short middle border to each short side of the quilt.
8. In the same manner, stitch 9 slices together to make a long middle border. Make 2.
9. Remove the stitches from the center of the remaining slice to make two short slices. Stitch a short slice to one end of each long middle border.
10. Stitch a 2 1/2" red print square to each end of the long middle borders. Stitch the borders to the long sides of the quilt.
11. Measure the length of the quilt including the borders. Trim 2 of the 5" x 96" dark purple print strips to that measurement and stitch them to the long sides of the quilt.
12. Trim the remaining 5" x 96" dark purple print strips to fit the quilt's width and stitch them to the remaining sides of the quilt.
13. Finish the quilt as described in the *General Directions*, using the 2 1/2" x 98" dark purple print strips for the binding. ◆

Dawn of a New Era
(continued from page 17)

4. Sew the blocks into rows and join the rows. Sew a corner triangle to each corner of the quilt.

5. Finish the quilt as described in the *General Directions*, using the 2 1/2" x 40" dark strips for the binding. ◆

Assembly Diagram

New York Beauty
(continued from page 21)

2. Stitch two 1 1/2" x 40" black strips and two 1 1/2" x 40" light gray strips together alternately, as shown. Make 2. Cut fifty-two 1 1/2" slices from the pieced strips.

3. Join 12 slices, end to end. Remove a gray square from the end of another slice and stitch the 3 remaining squares to the end of the strip to make an inner border. Make 4.

4. Stitch a dark D between a bright E and a bright ER make an outer border block. Make 48.

5. Stitch 12 outer border blocks together to make a border. Make 4.

6. Stitch an inner border to an outer border to make a pieced border. Make 4.

7. Stitch 2 pieced borders to opposite sides of the quilt.

8. Stitch a Corner Square to each end of the remaining pieced borders. Stitch them to the remaining sides of the quilt.

9. Finish the quilt according to the *General Directions,* using the 2 1/2" x 40" pink/orange strips for the binding. ◆

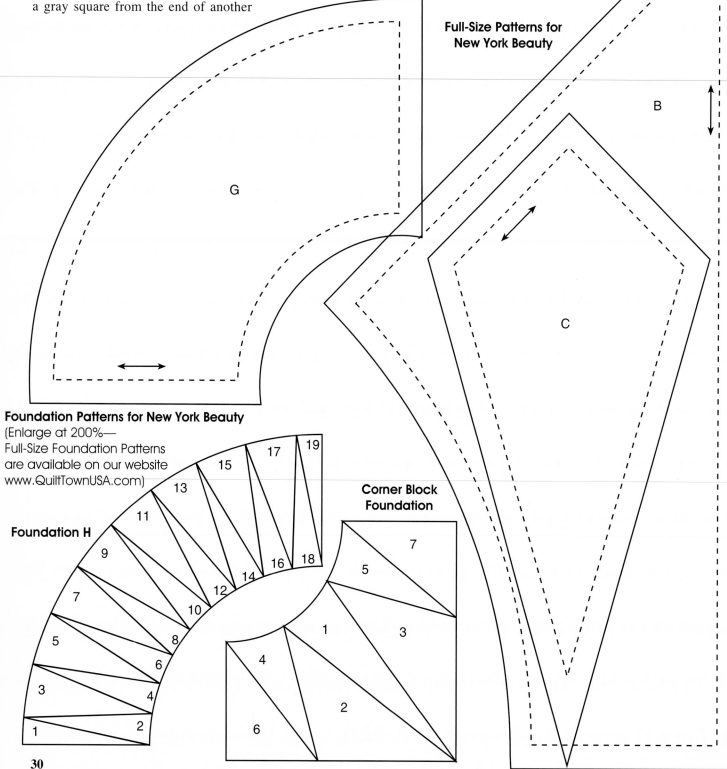

Full-Size Patterns for New York Beauty

G

B

C

Foundation Patterns for New York Beauty
(Enlarge at 200%—
Full-Size Foundation Patterns
are available on our website
www.QuiltTownUSA.com)

Foundation H

Corner Block Foundation

30

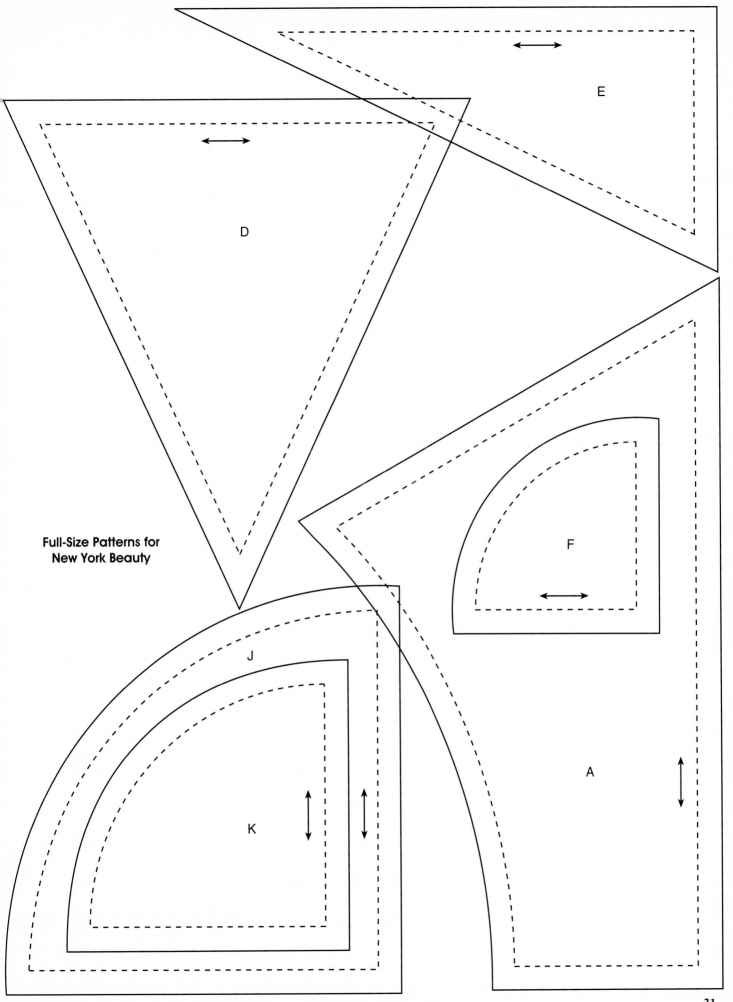

Full-Size Patterns for New York Beauty

E

D

F

J

K

A

General Directions

About the patterns

Read through the pattern directions before cutting fabric. Yardage requirements are based on fabric with a useable width of 40". Pattern directions are given in step-by-step order. If you are sending your quilt to a professional machine quilter, consult them regarding the necessary batting and backing size for your quilt. Batting and backing dimensions listed in the patterns are for hand quilting.

Fabrics

We suggest using 100% cotton. Wash fabric in warm water with mild detergent and no fabric softener. Dry fabric on a warm-to-hot setting. Press with a hot dry iron to remove any wrinkles.

Piecing

For machine piecing, sew 12 stitches per inch, exactly 1/4" from the edge of the fabric. To make accurate piecing easier, mark the throat plate with a piece of tape 1/4" to the right of the point where the needle pierces the fabric. Start and stop stitching at the cut edges except for set-in pieces. For set-ins, start and stop at the 1/4" seamline and backstitch.

For hand piecing, begin with a knot. Continue with a small running stitch, backstitching every 3-4 stitches. Stitch directly on the marked line from point to point, not edge to edge. Finish with 2 or 3 small backstitches before cutting the thread.

Foundation piecing

Foundation piecing is a method for making blocks with a high degree of accuracy. Foundation patterns need to be enlarged 200% and do not include a seam allowance. For each foundation, trace all of the lines and numbers onto paper. You will need one foundation for each block or part of a block as described in the pattern. The solid lines are stitching lines. The fabric pieces you select do not have to be cut precisely. Be generous when cutting fabric pieces as excess fabric will be trimmed away after sewing. Your goal is to cut a piece that covers the numbered area and extends into surrounding areas after seams are stitched. Generally, fabric pieces should be large enough to extend 1/2" beyond the seamline on all sides before stitching. For very small sections, or sections without angles, 1/4" may be sufficient.

Place fabric pieces on the unmarked side of the foundation and stitch on the marked side. Center the first piece, right side up, over position 1 on the unmarked side of the foundation. Hold the foundation up to a light to make sure that the raw edges of the fabric extend at least 1/2" beyond the seamline on all sides. Hold this first piece in place with a small dab of glue or a pin, as desired. Place the fabric for position 2 on the first piece, right sides together. Turn the foundation over, and sew on the line between 1 and 2, extending the stitching past the beginning and end of the line by a few stitches on both ends. Trim the seam allowance to 1/4". Fold the position 2 piece back, right side up, and press. Continue adding pieces to the foundation in the same manner until all positions are covered and the block is complete. Trim the fabric 1/4" beyond the edge of the foundation.

To avoid disturbing the stitches, do not remove the paper until the blocks have been joined together and at least one border has been added, unless instructed to remove them sooner in the pattern. The paper will be perforated from the stitching and can be gently pulled free. Use tweezers to carefully remove small sections of the paper, if necessary.

Mitered borders

Measure the length of the quilt top and add 2 times the border width plus 2". Cut border strips this measurement. Match the center of the quilt top with the center of the border strip and pin to the corners. Stitch, beginning, ending, and backstitching each seamline 1/4" from the edge of the quilt top. After all borders have been attached, miter one corner at a time. With the quilt top right side down, lay one border over the other. Draw a straight line at a 45° angle from the inner to the outer borders.

Reverse the positions of the borders and mark another corner-to-corner line. With the borders right sides together and the marked seamlines carefully matched, stitch from the inner to the outer corner, backstitching at each end. Open the mitered seam to make sure it lies flat, then trim excess fabric and press.

Finishing your quilt
Marking Quilting Designs

Mark before basting the quilt top together with the batting and backing. Chalk pencils show well on dark fabrics, otherwise use a very hard (#3 or #4) pencil or other marker for this purpose. Test your marker first.

Outline quilting does not require marking. Simply eyeball 1/4" from the seam or stitch "in the ditch" next to the seam. To prevent uneven stitching, try to avoid quilting through seam allowances whenever possible.

Basting

Cut the batting and backing at least 4" larger than the quilt top. Tape the backing, wrong side up, on a flat surface to anchor it. Smooth the batting on top, followed by the quilt top, right side up. Baste the three layers together to form a quilt sandwich. Begin at the center and baste horizontally, then vertically. Add more lines of basting approximately every 6" until the entire top is secured.

Quilting

Quilting is done with a short, strong needle called a "between." Use a thimble on the middle finger of the hand that pushes the needle. Begin quilting at the center of the quilt and work outward to keep the tension even and the quilting smooth.

Insert the needle through the quilt top and batting. Push the needle straight down into the quilt with the thimbled finger of the upper hand and slightly depress the fabric in front of the needle with the thumb. Redirect the needle back to the top of the quilt using the middle or index finger of the lower hand.

Repeat with each stitch using a rocking motion. Finish by knotting the thread close to the surface and popping the knot through the fabric to bury it. Remove basting when the quilting is complete.

If you wish to machine quilt, we recommend consulting one of the many fine books available on that subject.

Binding

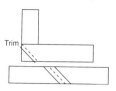

Cut the binding strips with the grain for straight-edge quilts. To make 1/2" finished binding, cut 2 1/2"-wide strips. Sew strips together with diagonal seam; trim and press seam allowance open.

Fold the strip in half lengthwise, wrong side in, and press. Position the strip on the right side of the quilt top, aligning the raw edges of the binding with the edge of the quilt top. Leaving 6" of the binding strip free and beginning a few inches from one corner, stitch the binding to the quilt with a 1/4" seam allowance measuring from the raw edge of the quilt top.

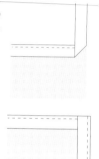

When you reach a corner, stop stitching 1/4" from the edge of the quilt top and backstitch. Clip the threads and remove the quilt from the machine. Fold the binding up and away from the quilt, forming a 45° angle, as shown.

Keeping the angled fold secure, fold the binding back down. This fold should be even with the edge of the quilt top. Begin stitching at the fold.

Continue stitching around the quilt in this manner to within 6" of the starting point. To finish, fold both strips back along the edge of the quilt so that the folded edges meet about 3" from both lines of the stitching and the binding lies flat on the quilt. Finger press to crease the folds. Measure the width of the folded binding. Cut the strips that distance beyond the folds. (In this case 1 1/4" beyond the folds.)

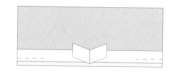

Open both strips and place the ends at right angles to each other, right sides together. Fold the bulk of the quilt out of your way. Join the strips with a diagonal seam as shown.

Trim the seam allowance to 1/4" and press it open. Refold the strip wrong side in. Place the binding flat against the quilt, and finish stitching it to the quilt. Trim excess batting and backing so that the binding edge will be filled with batting when you fold the binding to the back of the quilt. Blindstitch the binding to the back, covering the seamline.

Remove visible markings. Make a label that includes your name, the date the quilt was completed, and any other pertinent information, and stitch it to the back of your quilt. Sign and date your quilt.